Especially for

Melanie

From

Mom and Dad
with all our love
Date

April 23, 2011 on your
confirmation day.
x
We are so very proud
of the beautiful young woman
that you are.
May God bless you and keep you always.

Promises to *Soothe* Your Soul

{ Comforting Promises for Your Soul }

BARBOUR
PUBLISHING

Cover and interior illustrations: Todd Williams

Published by Barbour Publishing, Inc., P.O. Box 719, Uhrichsville, Ohio 44683, www.barbourbooks.com

Our mission is to publish and distribute inspirational products offering exceptional value and biblical encouragement to the masses.

Member of the
Evangelical Christian
Publishers Association

Printed in China.

Contents

Be Comforted!

*Praise be to the God and Father of our Lord Jesus Christ,
the Father of compassion and the God of all comfort,
who comforts us in all our troubles, so that we can comfort
those in any trouble with the comfort we ourselves
have received from God.*

2 CORINTHIANS 1:3–4 NIV

No matter what you face in this lifetime, God will be there
to wrap you in His loving embrace. This promise holds true—
in the good times and the bad. Ask God to soothe your soul
today. He'll reach out His comforting arms to you. That's a
promise you can count on!

Assurance

Why are you downcast, O my soul?
Why so disturbed within me? Put your hope in God,
for I will yet praise him, my Savior and my God.

PSALM 42:11 NIV

Ups and Downs

*I*n the book of Samuel, King David led the ark of the covenant to Jerusalem. "David and the whole house of Israel were celebrating with all their might before the LORD, with songs and with harps, lyres, tambourines, sistrums and cymbals" (2 Samuel 6:5 NIV). Such joy! Such confidence in God! Such harmony among the Israelites!

But skip forward to Psalm 42. David isn't singing or dancing or rejoicing anymore. In this lament he has to re-mind himself to hope in God. David's words sound wooden, forced. As if he is barely hanging on to his faith.

Aren't we just like David? Our journey of faith has ups and downs, great days and frustrating days. There are days when praising God is such a natural response. Some days we seem to soar. Joy bubbles up like a child's giggle.

Then there are days when God feels distant. Problems overwhelm us, and prayer feels a futile exercise, as if our pleas stop at the ceiling. There is no harmony in our homes, and we have little joy. Even worse, our confidence in God feels shaky.

Still, David reminds us to praise God. . .despite our doubts. Despite our discouragement. Despite the stack of problems that face us. For He is our Savior and our God!

~Suzanne Woods Fisher

What is meant by the peace that passes all understanding?
It does not mean a peace no one can comprehend. It means a
peace no amount of reasoning will bring. . . . Your heart can
rest in perfect security because God knows, He loves, He leads.

A. B. SIMPSON

An Awesome God

It is Your presence, Your blessings, Your love that makes my life so rich and fulfilling. I am not worried about what others have and I have not. I am full of joy for what I do have—mainly You! There is nothing greater than You, Lord. You are an awesome God. Nothing I do can make You any greater than Your Word and Your promises. I praise You for what You are doing in my life, for making me rich beyond my wildest dreams as I live and breathe in You.

~Donna Maltese

They shall mount up with wings as eagles.

ISAIAH 40:31 KJV

Of Growth

There is a fable about the way the birds got their wings at the beginning. They were first made without wings. Then God made the wings and put them down before the wingless birds and said to them, "Come, take up these burdens and bear them."

The birds had lovely plumage and sweet voices; they could sing, their feathers gleamed in the sunshine, but they could not soar in the air. They hesitated at first when bidden to take up the burdens that lay at their feet, but soon they obeyed; taking up the wings in their beaks, they laid them on their shoulders to carry them.

For a little while the load seemed heavy and hard to bear, but presently, as they went on carrying the burdens, folding them over their hearts, the wings grew fast to their little bodies. Soon they discovered how to use them and were lifted by them up into the air—the weights became wings.

The fable is a parable. We are the wingless birds, and our duties and tasks are the pinions God has made to lift us up and carry us heavenward. We look at our burdens and heavy loads and shrink from them, but as we lift them and bind them about our hearts, they become wings. On them we rise and soar toward God.

~Mrs. Charles E. Cowman

All God's glory and beauty come from within, and there He delights to dwell. His visits there are frequent, His conversation sweet, His comforts refreshing, His peace passing all understanding.

THOMAS À KEMPIS

I Look to You, Dear Lord

You are my hope, the Lord of my life. I wait on You and move cautiously in my decisions. I'm not ashamed to trust in Your guidance, Lord. Instead I feel thankful for the encouragement and surety You give me. As I trust in You, I'm filled with peace. Throughout the day my thoughts often turn to You for direction and strength. In quiet and confidence I find the strength only You can give.

You, dear Father, are my Rock and my Defender; I shall not fear. I know in whom I believe, and I'm persuaded that You keep me close to You day by day.

I look to You. I doubt not in Your unfailing love for me. Thank You.

In Jesus' name. Amen.

~Anita Corrine Donihue

My flesh and my heart may fail, but God is the strength of my heart and my portion forever.

PSALM 73:26 NIV

Blessings

In the day of prosperity be joyful, but in the day of adversity consider: Surely God has appointed the one as well as the other, so that man can find out nothing that will come after him.

ECCLESIASTES 7:14 NKJV

Always Blessed

Sometimes our souls don't feel particularly satisfied. If we lose a job, wonder how we'll pay the rent, and imagine all kinds of dire results, it's hard to feel very peaceful. Prosperous days seem to lie behind us, and we can't look into the future and tell how long we'll be in this situation.

God doesn't allow us to look into the future. That's a good thing, because if we knew the future, we wouldn't need to trust God. One of His best methods of developing our spiritual lives would no longer exist, and we'd enter heaven as weak, spineless beings, not the strong ones He wants to create.

But just as God ordained good things in our prosperous times, He brings good even from our most challenging moments. Unemployment may provide a time for spiritual deepening in many ways, as we cling more firmly to Him and know that all we receive comes directly from His hand. When our days are not filled with work at an office or shop, some temporary ministry may appear.

But whether we are joyful or sad, God still remains faithful. He provides for our needs, even if we don't get the lavish things we'd prefer. And He always provides generous spiritual blessings for those who trust in Him. Like Paul, who experienced prosperity and want, we can do all things when we abound in Him (Philippians 4:12–13).

No matter what your circumstances, you can always cling to Jesus—and be blessed.

~Pamela McQuade

21

The sun. . .in its full glory, either at rising or setting—this, and many other like blessings we enjoy daily; and for the most of them, because they are so common, most men forget to pay their praises. But let not us.

IZAAK WALTON

A Daily Benediction

*M*ay You walk down the road with me today. May You shower my path with Your many blessings. May You keep me from danger. May Your light keep me from the darkness surrounding me. May You give me grace and peace and strength for the day. May You give me someone to bless as You have blessed me. May You be there, waiting for me, at the end of the day, with a good word to calm my spirit as I rest in Your arms.

~Donna Maltese

"If you keep quiet at a time like this, deliverance and relief for the Jews will arise from some other place, but you and your relatives will die. Who knows if perhaps you were made queen for just such a time as this?"

ESTHER 4:14 NLT

Beyond the Blessing

When her cousin Mordecai asked Esther to stand up for her people, the queen had a lot to lose. Her husband had already gotten rid of one queen who displeased him, and this young, beautiful woman could even lose her life. Yet after Mordecai reminded her that God was still in control, she approached the king about the wrongdoing of his favorite, Haman, and ended up saving her people. The king entirely supported her.

Like Esther, we find ourselves in difficult situations. We may not be threatened with loss of life or position, but maybe it's a job or promotion we'll have to bypass. Perhaps we fear that we'll ruin a relationship that may be rocky but at least exists; we'd prefer not to lose it entirely.

But when God places a challenge before us, it's never because He plans on deserting us. As with Esther, He may open the ears of those who listen to our plight. Or if they won't listen, He provides an even better workplace or friendship. Nothing that we lose because we obey God will ruin our lives.

God's still in control of every situation, every emotion, and every human thought. The universe belongs to Him, including all the people in it. At such a time as this, He may be planning something wonderful, a step beyond the problem. Just because we don't see the blessing yet doesn't mean it isn't on its way.

~Pamela McQuade

Be on the lookout for mercies. The more we look for them, the more of them we will see. Blessings brighten when we count them.

MALTBIE D. BABCOCK

Well-Watered Gardens

You are the source of my life. Day by day You have met my needs in this sun-scorched land afflicted with the heat of greed and intolerance. As I come to You with today's petitions, may I be reminded of the ways You have rescued me in the past, resting in the assurance that You will once again deliver me from my troubles. Right now, in Your presence, I feel Your life springing up within me. Thank You for Your living water that never fails.

~Donna Maltese

May He grant you according to your heart's desire, and fulfill all your purpose.

PSALM 20:4 NKJV

Contentment

Whosoever shall not receive the kingdom of God as a little child shall in no wise enter therein.

LUKE 18:17 KJV

30

As Peaceful as a Flower

We complicate our lives when we borrow trouble from the future. We waste our energy worrying about what might happen tomorrow; we become frantic and pressured looking at the many responsibilities on our to-do list for the next week; we lie awake obsessing over our plans for the upcoming month.

And meanwhile we miss the precious gift of peace that God has given us right here, right now, in this tiny present moment that touches eternity. Be like the wildflowers, Jesus tells us in the Gospels, simply soaking up today's sunshine: "Take therefore no thought for the morrow: for the morrow shall take thought for the things of itself" (Matthew 6:34 KJV).

Children live the same way, delighting in the here and now, untroubled by the future. When we can find that same wholehearted simplicity, we, too, will know the peace of God's kingdom.

~Ellyn Sanna

Let your strivings, then, be after contentment. Get out of each passing day all the sweetness there is in it. Live in the present hour as much as possible, and if you live for character, your foundations will outlast tomorrow.

GEORGE H. HEPWORTH

Change My Thoughts

Lord, I don't want to be like the people of this world, running around at breakneck speed, trying to multitask until I'm so deep in the darkness I can no longer see the light of Your face. It's not all about doing; it's about being. Change my way of thinking to Your way of thinking. I take this to-do list and place it in Your capable hands. Help me to see this list through Your eyes. Show me clearly the steps I am to take today.

~Donna Maltese

33

Let us lay aside every weight. . .let us run with patience the race that is set before us.

HEBREWS 12:1 KJV

34

Make Room for Peace

Our society is a busy one. As we dash from responsibility to responsibility, we seem to pride ourselves on our busyness, as though it somehow proves our worth. Even our children are busy, their schedules crammed with enriching activities. We all fly through life, fitting as many things as we can into each day.

With such complicated lives, it's no wonder we find our hearts craving quiet. We long for it so much that books on peace and simplicity climb the bestseller lists; we're all hoping some author will have the magic answer that will show us how to infuse our lives with serenity.

But we're looking at peace as though it were one more thing to fit into our lives, as though we could write it on our to-do list. (There it is, right between *Take the dog to the vet* and *Pick up the clothes from the dry cleaner*: *Find a little peace*.) But the truth is, that's not the way peace works.

The only way we will find peace in the midst of our hectic lives is if we make room for it. When we stop the mad rush, when we say no to some of our many responsibilities and take the time to come quietly into God's presence, then, in that simple, quiet moment, He will breathe His peace into our hearts.

~Ellyn Sanna

They who are God's without reserve are in every situation
content, for they will do only what He wills and desire
to do for Him whatever He desires them to do and be.
They strip themselves of everything and in this nakedness
find all things restored one hundredfold.

CHARLES SPURGEON

The Power of Contentment

Oh Lord, I feel as if I have it all. With You in my life, I need not worry about anything. For as You dress the flowers that neither toil nor spin and feed the birds that neither sow nor reap, You shall do even more for me. I do not worry about what I will eat, wear, drink, or earn today; I leave all my concerns in Your hands, knowing that You will provide. You are first in my life.

~Donna Maltese

You, LORD, give true peace to those who depend on you, because they trust you.

ISAIAH 26:3 NCV

Faith

For our light affliction, which is but for a moment,
worketh for us a far more exceeding
and eternal weight of glory.

2 CORINTHIANS 4:17 KJV

Take Comfort

Do you ever feel your trials are like wearing a crown of thorns? Be faithful. As you trust in God, your crown of thorns will be taken away and He will hand you a crown with stars instead. Remember to thank and praise Him.

Do you feel like you are overloaded, your hands filled with heavy cares? Be faithful. As you keep trusting in God, He will take away your heavy cares and place a harp in your grasp, so you may sing glory and honor to God for all He has done. Remember to thank and praise Him.

Do your garments feel soiled with dirt and grime from struggling in a sin-sick world? Stay faithful. He will replace them with clothing that is shining white. Remember to thank and praise Him.

Hold on and do not despair. There will be a time when you look back and your trials will seem as nothing in light of the many answered prayers, miracles, and evidence of God's glory and grace.

Step-by-step, day by day, He takes each trial and turns it inside out. Triumphs emerge like a marvelous spiritual metamorphosis. Each of your obedient acts will be transformed to joy unspeakable!

So take heart. Stay faithful. When all is ever so dark, know for sure morning follows the night.

When the dawn breaks through, remember to lift your heart in thanksgiving and praise to the One who gives all comfort and help.

~Anita Corrine Donihue

Faith is to believe what we do not see;
and the reward of this faith is
to see what we believe.

Augustine

Strengthened in the Faith

*J*esus, my Jesus, thank You for always being with me, holding me up above the waters of this life, especially when the current is more than I can bear. As You uphold me, day by day, morning by morning, my faith grows. There is no one like You, Jesus. *No one like You*. I am strengthened during this time with You. I overflow with goodness and praise. What would I ever do without You in my life?

~Donna Maltese

Jesus answered and said unto them,
Verily I say unto you, If ye have faith,
and doubt not, ye shall not only do this
which is done to the fig tree, but also if ye
shall say unto this mountain, Be thou
removed, and be thou cast into the
sea; it shall be done.

MATTHEW 21:21 KJV

Believe Your Father

You are no more under a necessity to be doubtful as to your relationship to your heavenly Father than you are to be doubtful as to your relationship to your earthly father. In both cases the thing you must depend on is their word, not your feelings; and no earthly father has ever declared or manifested his fatherhood in one-thousandth part as unmistakably or as lovingly as your heavenly Father has declared and manifested His. If you would not "make God a liar," therefore, you must make your believing as inevitable and necessary a thing as your obedience. You would obey God, I believe, even though you should die in the act. Believe Him, also, even though the effort to believe should cost you your life. The conflict may be very severe; it may seem at times unendurable. But let your unchanging declaration be from henceforth, "Though he slay me, yet will I trust in him" (Job 13:15 KJV). When doubts come, meet them, not with arguments but with assertions of faith. All doubts are an attack of the enemy; the Holy Spirit never suggests them, never. He is the Comforter not the Accuser, and He never shows us our need without at the same time revealing the divine supply.

~Hannah Whitall Smith

45

Faith is an outward look. Faith does not look within; it looks without. It is not what I think, nor what I feel, nor what I have done, but it is what Jesus Christ is and has done; and so we should trust in Him who is our strength, and whose strength will never fail.

DWIGHT L. MOODY

In Everything I Praise You

*Y*our decisions for my life are right, O Lord, for You are my Father. You care for me. You are the Potter. Shape me as You would. Teach me Your lessons, that I may be worthy of being Your child. Help me to be pliable clay so You can form me the way You please. I have no fear of Your plan, Lord. Instead I put my trust completely in You.

I may not understand why things happen the way they do. I may even cry out in difficult times, when I don't see the reasoning of it all. Yet I will let You purify me in Your loving way.

Make me like silver and gold as you refine me and skim away the dross and impurities. At times this is difficult, but I must trust You and obey because You know what is best for me.

When the trials come, help me draw closer to You. I know You, Lord Jesus, suffered, too. Through each struggle I will strive to remain true. Afterward, as You have promised, I will share again the wonderful joy You have waiting for me.

I praise You in everything, Lord, that the will of God will be accomplished through me.

~Anita Corrine Donihue

47

"I am the resurrection and the life.
He who believes in me will live,
even though he dies; and whoever
lives and believes in me will never die.
Do you believe this?"

John 11:25–26 niv

God's Love

If ye had known me, ye should have known my Father also: and from henceforth ye know him, and have seen him.

JOHN 14:7 KJV

No Fear

A friend of mine told me her childhood was passed in a perfect terror of God. Her idea of Him was that He was a cruel giant with an awful "eye" which could see everything, no matter how it might be hidden, and that He was always spying upon her, and watching for chances to punish her, and to snatch away all her joys.

With a child's strange reticence, she never told anyone of her terror; but one night, Mother, coming into the room unexpectedly, heard the poor little despairing cry, and, with a sudden comprehension of what it meant, sat down beside the bed, and, taking the cold little hand in hers, told her God was not a dreadful tyrant to be afraid of, but was just like Jesus; and that she knew how good and kind Jesus was, and how He loved little children and took them in His arms and blessed them. My friend said she had always loved the stories about Jesus, and when she heard that God was like Him, it was a perfect revelation to her and took away her fear of God forever. She went about all that day saying to herself over and over, "Oh, I am so glad I have found out that God is like Jesus, for Jesus is so nice. Now I need never be afraid of God anymore."

The little child had got a sight of God "in the face of Jesus Christ," and it brought rest to her soul.

~Hannah Whitall Smith

God is everything that is good and comfortable for us.
He is our clothing that for love wraps us, clasps us,
and all surrounds us for tender love.

JULIAN OF NORWICH

Loved Now and Forever

No matter what happens, Lord, I cannot be separated from You and Your love. Oh what that means to me! Fill me with the love that never ends. May it flow through me and reach those I meet this day. May my future be filled with blessing upon blessing, and may I praise You today and in the days to come.

~Donna Maltese

For God so loved the world, that he
gave his only begotten Son.

JOHN 3:16 KJV

54

The Unselfishness of God

On the flyleaf of my Bible, I find the following words, taken from I know not where: "This generation has rediscovered the unselfishness of God."

If I am not mistaken, the generation before mine knew very little of the unselfishness of God; and, even of my own generation, there are, I fear, many good and earnest Christians who do not know it yet. Without putting it into such words as to shock themselves or others, many Christians still at the bottom look upon God as one of the most selfish, self-absorbed beings in the universe, far more selfish than they could think it right to be themselves, intent only upon His own honor and glory, looking out continually that His own rights are never trampled on, and so absorbed in thoughts of Himself and of His own righteousness as to have no love or pity to spare for the poor sinners who have offended Him.

To discover that He is not the selfish being we are so often apt to think Him, but is instead really and fundamentally unselfish, caring not at all for Himself, but only and always for us and for our welfare, is to have found the answer to every human question, and the cure for every human ill.

~Hannah Whitall Smith

We are so preciously loved by God that we cannot
even comprehend it. No created being can
ever know how much and how sweetly
and tenderly God loves them.

JULIAN OF NORWICH

I Dedicate My Heart to You

*F*ather, I give You my heart, my soul, my life. I dedicate my whole being to You. I give You my failures and my successes, my fears and my aspirations.

Search my heart. Let my thoughts and motives be pure. You know me through and through. Remove the unclean ways in me that I might be pleasing to You.

Fill me with Your Spirit, I pray; enable me to do the tasks set before me. Lead me into Your everlasting way.

Wherever I go, whatever the challenge, I pray that You will be there, guiding me completely. From my rising in the morn to my resting at night, O Lord, be near, surrounding me continually with Your love.

I look forward with joyful anticipation to what You have planned for me. Thank You for becoming Lord of my life.

~Anita Corrine Donihue

We have known and believed the love that God has for us. God is love, and he who abides in love abides in God, and God in him.

I JOHN 4:16 NKJV

Grace

Therefore, there is now no condemnation
for those who are in Christ Jesus.

ROMANS 8:1 NIV

Condemnation versus Conviction

*Y*ou are a loser. You can't do anything right. You will never be forgiven. Condemning words pierce our hearts and knock the wind right out of us. They are difficult to overcome. They prevent us from moving forward. Whether shouted in our ear or whispered to our heart, their source is the same. Condemning words originate with Satan. Their purpose is to drive us further away from God by making us feel unloved, unworthy, and hopeless.

Convicting words—*You are worthy and precious*, *You can do all things through Christ*, and *You are forgiven*—on the other hand, have a completely different tone. They originate with the Holy Spirit with the purpose of drawing us closer to God. Although correction and rebuke may be needed, love is always present. Acknowledging our sin is a prerequisite to receiving God's grace and forgiveness. When God's love is experienced in the form of discipline, restoration and freedom are the results.

As believers we are never condemned because Jesus Christ paid the penalty for sin once and for all when He died on the cross. So, when condemning words stop us in our tracks, we need to stand on truth. Then move toward the God who always loves, forgives, and yearns for a close relationship with us.

~Julie Rayburn

The Lord's chief desire is to reveal Himself to you, and,
in order for Him to do that, He gives you abundant grace.
The Lord gives you the experience of enjoying His presence.
He touches you, and His touch is so delightful that,
more than ever, you are drawn inwardly to Him.

MADAME JEANNE GUYON

With All That Is within Me

Everything I am, all that is within me, I draw upon as I praise Your holy name. You have done so many great things and have given me the power to do even greater things as I allow You to live through me. Thank You for healing me, for forgiving me. You are an awesome God!

~Donna Maltese

You therefore, my son, be strong in the
grace that is in Christ Jesus.

2 TIMOTHY 2:1 NKJV

Strength in Grace

The young mother watched her child take his first hesitant steps. After tumbling to the ground, he turned to his mother, seeking her reaction. Her bright smile and obvious joy at his success, not his fall, encouraged the child to try again. Each time he tried, he grew stronger. Before long, the child's steps were no longer hesitant, but confident.

By not displaying anger or concern, but showing understanding and encouragement, the mother gave her son the strength to climb back up and try again. The boy trusted her for his well-being. He continued to learn to walk and then to run.

As Christians we often fall or make mistakes. God's grace is always there to demonstrate His forgiveness. He urges us to climb to our feet and try again. Every time we attempt to walk in faith, we are resting in God's grace and drawing strength from Him. On our own, we would fall and not be able to try again. With God in charge of our well-being, we can not only have the ability to walk, but we can learn to run with confidence in God.

~Nancy Farrier

Grace is no stationary thing; it is ever becoming. It is flowing straight out of God's heart. Grace does nothing but re-form and convey God. Grace makes the soul conformable to the will of God. God, the ground of the soul, and grace go together.

MEISTER ECKHART

I Want to Be Like Jesus

*L*ord, I know that You will work everything out according to Your glory, according to Your will. I feel privileged that You have chosen me to serve You, that You have called me to this life. I want to be like You. Give me the strength of Christ, for His grace is sufficient for me. Thank You for hearing my prayer. O my soul, rejoice!

~Donna Maltese

How rich is God's grace, which he has given to us so fully and freely.

EPHESIANS 1:7–8 NCV

Prayer

Do not be anxious about anything,
but in everything, by prayer and petition,
with thanksgiving, present your requests to God.

PHILIPPIANS 4:6 NIV

Compelled to Pray

$\mathcal{I}$ don't go very long without a diet soft drink in my hand. When I feel the need for something to drink, nothing gets in my way until my thirst is quenched.

In the same way, sometimes my soul feels so dry that I long to drink in the soothing, soul-quenching grace of the Holy Spirit. The need becomes so strong that I drop what I'm doing and slip away to a private place—the bedroom, the bathroom, or the back porch.

When I go to my Father, I am never disappointed. He reveals to me my innermost self. He shows me the burdens that I thought I had laid at His feet but which I later took back upon myself. He reminds me of the needs of others that perhaps I had promised to pray for but didn't. He listens as I confess what He already knew. He restores my soul.

One of my favorite verses is "For it is God who works in you to will and to act according to his good purpose" (Philippians 2:13 NIV). When I have a longing to pray, it's not because of anything I've done. . .but because my Creator is moving in me. What an awesome thought! It never ceases to amaze me that God actually takes the time to notice insignificant me and to draw me closer to Him. What's even more amazing is that to God I'm not insignificant at all. In fact, even when the whole world may be against me, my Lord thinks I'm pretty special. Wow, what a Savior!

~Leigh Ann Thomas

More things are wrought by prayer
than this world dreams of.

ALFRED, LORD TENNYSON

Christ's Riches

Oh Lord, what a promise You have made to me, that You will supply all I need through Christ. He is my Good Shepherd; with Him I shall not want! Help me to rest confidently in the assurance that in Your time my prayers will be answered. Let my prayer time be more than utterances of what I desire but a time of fellowship with You, knowing that You will provide what I need.

~Donna Maltese

The LORD hath heard my supplication:
the LORD will receive my prayer.

PSALM 6:9 KJV

Peace in Prayer

God doesn't want us to worry, get stressed out, or be bothered. So He offers a solution to those states of mind: prayer. He reminds us—there's nothing He won't be happy to help us with, if only we mention it to Him.

Maybe we think we don't need to bother God with something "this small." He'd be glad to help with anything, even the tiniest problem. Nothing is below the notice of Him who created subatomic particles. Or maybe we figure we don't need help on this one. He'll be there to share the good things, and if unexpected trouble comes up, He'll be happy to assist us, too.

God's trying to tell us He wants to be a part of every moment of our lives. Whether it's something we simply need to mention or a deep concern we petition for a long time, He's interested.

Only when we give Him all our anxieties can He have the kind of impact on our lives—and on the lives of others to whom we minister—He's always had in mind. Then we'll also experience two unexpected benefits: thanksgiving and peace. We'll appreciate what our Savior begins to give and offer Him thanks, deepening and expanding our trust relationship. As we do that, harmony will fill our lives.

Find peace in prayer today.

~Pamela McQuade

In our daily practice of prayer,
we should begin each day
with an act of loving thankfulness to God.

C. F. ANDREWS

Sharing Abundance

*L*ord, as I present my needs to You and as You meet those needs, remind me of the needs of others, realizing that I may be Your answer to someone else's prayer today.

~Donna Maltese

"You will call upon me and come and pray to me, and I will listen to you. You will seek me and find me when you seek me with all your heart."

JEREMIAH 29:12—13 NIV

Rest

News about Jesus kept spreading. Large crowds came to listen to him teach and to be healed of their diseases. But Jesus would often go to some place where he could be alone and pray.

LUKE 5:15—16 CEV

Calgon, Take Me Away!

Several years ago the Calgon company aired a commercial portraying a frantic, busy mom in her chaotic home. Kids are yelling, dogs are barking, the phone is ringing, and it is apparent that she is past her limit! She utters that still-famous line, "Calgon, take me away!" and she is instantly soaking in a luxurious bubble bath, in a silent bathroom.

Even Jesus needed escape from the chaos of constantly having throngs of people around Him. He needed to find a quiet place to pray and think. That doesn't make Him a bad Friend or Master; it simply proves that He, the Son of God, was also human. He knew the importance of protecting Himself both mentally and emotionally.

We need to be sure to get our Calgon moments. It doesn't make us bad or insensitive to others. We must find that quiet place to be alone with our thoughts and spend time in reflection and prayer. The chaos of life is often too loud to hear the Savior's voice. By seeking out silence, we will be better able to hear Him when He calls.

~Nicole O'Dell

81

Drop Thy still dews of quietness,
Till all our strivings cease;
Take from our souls the strain and stress,
And let our ordered lives confess
The beauty of Thy peace.

JOHN G. WHITTIER

Quiet Waters

My Shepherd, my Lord, my Savior, lead me beside the still waters. Lie with me in the green pastures. Restore my soul. Lead me down the paths of Your choosing today. With You by my side, I fear no evil. You are my Comfort and my Guide. I am happy in Your presence. Your goodness and Your mercy are with me this minute, this hour, this day. Thank You, Lord, for leading me here and making me whole—for being the Shepherd of my life.

~Donna Maltese

The LORD replied, "My Presence will go with you, and I will give you rest."

EXODUS 33:14 NIV

Rest for the Weary

*L*abor comes in so many varieties. We labor to bring in an income; to pray daily and study the Word; to meet the spiritual needs of others; and to be good parents, children, or grandparents. Often we feel overwhelmed by all we must accomplish in a day.

When we feel that way, there is a solution—as He did for Moses, God offers to take up our burdens and give us much-needed relief. As we simply cling to this promise, He gives us rest.

But it's up to us to go to the Lord with our needs. Often we get so caught up in trying to find our own solutions, we simply don't tell Him about them. It's as if we assume He knows, so we need not talk about it. But we forget that God doesn't barge into our lives. As long as we hold on to finding our own solutions to what overwhelms us, He'll let us lose our way in our own efforts.

If we take advantage of His offer and come to Him, everything changes. When we place a trouble in God's hands then take His advice, seemingly insolvable problems slip away or are lightened by our sharing them with the Savior. It's not magic but a sweet release.

Working hard on our own, we create only stress, worry, and more uncertainty. Only resting in Him brings the answer to every need.

~Pamela McQuade

When God finds a soul that rests in Him and is not easily moved, He operates within it in His own manner. That soul allows God to do great things within it. He gives to [it] the key to the treasures He has prepared for it so that it might enjoy them. And to this same soul He gives the joy of His presence.

CATHERINE OF GENOA

From Calamity to Calm

*F*ather, this day has too much responsibility for me. My head spins with frustration. My life is full of calamity. Help me to gain Your perspective. When my footing begins to slip, let me cling to You, my Fortress. Instill Your direction in my cluttered mind. When I am weak, lend me Your quiet, confident strength; when impatient, grant me Your patience. If I fail, help me not to keep punishing myself but to leave it in Your hands and go on.

Teach me to eliminate those things that are unnecessary and to concentrate on the essentials. Help me slow down enough to take time for myself and You.

Keep my thoughts accurate, my hands sure, and my feet swift in doing Your will. Remind me of my limitations, Lord. Keep my step close behind—not in front of—You, and protect me with Your strong hands.

At the day's end I will lie down and reflect on all I have learned. I will recall how much You have helped me. I will praise You with great joy as I drift to sleep nestled in the protection of Your mighty wings.

~Anita Corrine Donihue

[Jesus said]: "Are you tired? Worn out? Burned out on religion? Come to me. Get away with me and you'll recover your life. I'll show you how to take a real rest."

MATTHEW 11:28 MSG

Time

The Lord is not slow in keeping his promise, as some understand slowness. He is patient with you, not wanting anyone to perish, but everyone to come to repentance.

2 PETER 3:9 NIV

Define Slow

Time may drag as you're waiting for God to aid you in changing a bad habit or to bring newness to a difficult relationship. You begin to wonder if He'll ever intervene. Then when you least expect it, He brings wonderful change into your life. Was God slow? No, He just had another plan, and when the time was perfect, He did what you'd asked for.

It's the same, Peter told his readers, with the day of the Lord, the time when Jesus will return for His people. Because it hadn't happened on these first-century believers' schedule, they began to doubt the promise. When nonbelievers scoffed at their faith, the Christians asked, "Why is God so slow?"

Peter assured them God had not forgotten His people or His promise. He simply had a better plan—one that would add many others to their kingdom. As it turned out, Jesus didn't return during their century. But that doesn't mean He wasn't faithful. Though the early Christians might have been stunned that God would wait so long, they couldn't have argued with the need for many others to come to Him.

It's all a matter of how we define *slow*. If it means "anything that doesn't fit into our schedules," we *would* consider God slow. But if it means "something behind God's schedule," the word can't be used about God's plan. He's never behind on His own timetable. So no, God isn't slow in coming—or in doing anything else in our lives. The real question is: Are we on God's schedule or our own?

~Pamela McQuade

91

Time, indeed, is a sacred gift,
and each day is a little life.

SIR JOHN LUBBOCK

In His Time

Lord, sometimes I don't understand why it takes so long for You to answer some of my prayers. At times Your answers are immediate, but on other occasions I need to keep coming before You, asking over and over again for You to meet my need. Help me to grow during this time, Lord. Give me the confidence to ask and keep on asking.

~Donna Maltese

The LORD is good to those who wait for Him,
to the soul who seeks Him.

LAMENTATIONS 3:25 NKJV

Patient Waiting

*N*one of us gets every expectation fulfilled by God in a moment. All of us wait on Him at times that may seem painful or inconvenient to us. But as we're waiting, do we understand that this, too, can be God's goodness?

Waiting to find a mate can be difficult—I know that from experience. But I decided that marrying the right person—God's person—was better than suffering through a divorce with the wrong person. And wait I did. How long? Let's just put it this way: Anyone who feels that waiting until twenty-five to marry is too long just hasn't begun to wait, if that's God's will.

As the years went by, I was tempted to think I'd done something wrong. I wondered if I had some huge character flaw that no one was willing to share with me. One older friend asked if all the men in my state were blind. Still I waited, patiently praying, seeking to obey God's will for my work and spiritual life. When my social life seemed empty, I still hung on.

Finally, about the time I decided no one was coming, I met my husband, who had also been faithfully waiting. We didn't marry at the usual age but in God's perfect timing. Many problems that might have endangered our relationship, if we'd married earlier, had already been dealt with. God had been good to us, though we hadn't understood it all those years.

If you, too, are waiting on God's timing, do so patiently. Trust that it's all for your good, and you'll find, in the end, that it was.

~Pamela McQuade

We walk without fear, full of hope and courage and strength to do His will, waiting for the endless good which He is always giving as fast as He can get us able to take it in.

George MacDonald